Spare Parts

Spare Parts

A Novella in Verse

Anne Harding Woodworth

Turning Point

Published by Turning Point
P.O. Box 541106
Cincinnati, OH 45254-1106

ISBN: 9781934999318
LCCN: 2008908966

Poetry Editor: Kevin Walzer
Business Editor: Lori Jareo

Visit us on the web at www.turningpointbooks.com

for Fred

"There's no one who scares
me when I see them in my mirror."

—Dale Earnhardt, *Sporting News*

Contents

Spare Parts

1 *In which Lacey offers a setting, high and low, old world and new*

When you come from the mountains or come from the hills,
even the hills of Tennessee, no flat moves you
except if you see it from a ridge or a pass
or an airplane you jump from and land so that you
walk where marsh once drenched earth and now cotton grows tame.
Over Levadia's plain in Greece—circling 'round
like that, you land, get dragged, walk back to the mountains.

The going up is easy though knee cartilage
is frayed like shoelaces, awning rope. It's the walk
down that's hard because your feet and ankles push up
into your shins into your knees into your heart
cavity, shoulders, neck, the wheeze of your throat, your
pituitary. Juices burn, they don't relent
for your pain, familiar pain of common descent.

That's Paul, not me. Oh, no. My knees are fine. Just fine.

The house next door is the color of dead leaves, oak
and tulip trees, clapboards like loose bark, roof slanting
both ways, shingled, sparkling with black and gray cinders
and copper flashing 'round the stone chimney that smoked

white on cold nights before Sybil died and husband
Gaddis was left free to try on her dresses, all
of her jackets, and look into the mirror with
a comfort at last, relief he'd not known before.
I know he loved her, he did, I'm so sure of that,
and once I saw him kiss the face in the mirror
tearful in the early days of widowership.

2 *In which Gaddis reflects on mirror images*

Paul was an insurance salesman,
took to it like fish to water,
knew terms like liabilities
indemnities, and acts of God,

which always seemed to me to be
arbitrary, temporary,
imaginary. Yet isn't
everything imaginary?

I imagine me in mirrors,
glass that reflects vision less than
truthful, passing right for left, left
right. Opposites bespeak only

those appearances and seemings,
never in those verbs of being.

3 *In which Paul remembers his Ford Galaxie*

When I was a kid, nothing was truer
than my 1960 Galaxie, sleek
sled, maroon and chrome, with leather-covered

power seats. Equipped with power steering,
it had Cruise-O-Matic, spotlight mirror,
automotive parts a guy would die for.

Galaxie Starliner hardtop two-door—
it took me and countless other guys from
carhop to drive-in movies, its long, low

oil pan, one of many secrets under
its hood, this V-eight that came my way through
no effort of my own, but rather when

an uncle "bought the farm," as I would put
it in those days of callous disregard
for the fragility of breath. He chose

me as his next of kin, no lover, wife
to whom he might have bequeathed his estate
consisting of a car and pair of shoes.

With my friend Gaddis I drove the mountains
in search of girls, races, cigarettes, booze,
deserted roads for drag strips by the moon.

This car, this set of wheels that carried me
into ecstasy I'd not known before,
was my religion, my identity.

4 *In which Gaddis begins to explain himself*

My name is Andrew Gaddis Tish.
They call me Gaddis, my mother's
maiden name. She died giving birth
to me. Her rich dad made dead sure

they'd call me Gaddis, which became
Gladys by third grade, but I was
never bothered, kind of fancied
it—in secret in the attic

where I'd go to be alone, where
one day—I was eight or nine—I
opened up a trunk where I found
face down my mama's wedding gown.

I pulled the zipper slowly down
the back, gently took the shoulders
and held them up against myself.
Every attic's mirror awaits

that one stalwart occasion when
it proves it still can do its job.
And sure enough our smudged and dusty
glass showed me a bride to love.

I slipped the dress over my head
and zipped it up, a dress too big
but smooth as skin. I later learned
to call it *peau de soie*, an apt

name for the off-white silky gown
I wore that day. I also found
my mother's shoes, size 8, high heels.
I slid my feet, size 1, within.

And then the veil. My hair was much
too trim to hold the tortoise combs,
but I laid the tulle on my head,
brownish tulle that flowed to my shins.

There I stood before the mirror,
smiling at my loveliness when—
"Gaddis?" My dad was coming up.
"Are you up here? I've been calling,

son, are you up . . . " He stopped at
the top of the stairs, staring at me.
I looked at him, no word sounded.
Then my father picked me up, put

his head against my neck. I felt
his tears descending into
the scoop neck of the dress. Quietly,
he carried me downstairs to his

reading chair, and there began to
read to me "The Cremation of
Sam McGee," which I learned by heart.
And ever since, I've linked to it

the day my father let go of
the woman of his life and took
me into his universe, me,
his first and lonely son in search

of him, a father and a man.

5 *In which Gaddis contemplates Paul's Galaxie, Bristol Speedway, Brenda Lee, and college*

In the solitude of childhood
I had a pal. His name was Paul.
He lived next door and never called
me Gladys, indoctrinated

me in girls and sports, though strangely,
while I ran tight end for our school,
Paul played soccer, which all the less
athletic types did in those days,

but any extra time was spent
on Paul's maroon and glass-packed Ford.
He loved that car, that Galaxie,
low-to-ground muffler sound that filled

the Appalachians more than fog.
Paul taught me everything there was
to know or learn about stock cars
and the combustion engine, gas,

the carburetor, oil and spark,
about disparate spare parts,

original and after-market,
that went into making up his

Galaxie. Naturally we'd
never heard of catalytic
converters, intermittent wipers,
or of digital computers,

But we knew about Daytona.
No speedway had come to Bristol
yet, "twin" city, part-Virginia,
part-Tennessee. Saturdays we'd

find a six-pack with I.D. of
doubtful authenticity, but
such is that pat complicity
between friends.

The spring we finished
high school, Bristol got its speedway.
Paul and I went to the first race,
July three-oh, with Brenda Lee's

"Oh, say, can you see?"—Brenda Lee!
seventeen, like us, yet she seemed
so mature, we talked about her,
dreamed about her till summer's end

when off at universities,
we broke bonds temporarily—
me to UT, while Paul went north
to the State of Massachusetts.

At UT a certain girl named
Sybil sat right next to me in
botany where we learned about
pine trees and cotton plants, seeds of

southern soils, how they grow, how they
reproduce, how oils, resins form,
xylems, phloems, photosynthesis,
how brightly shone the sun on me.

This gave me a start in growing
cotton, which led to threads, which led
to nylon monofilament,
which led to molding plastic spools.

How strange the course that chooses us—
from nature to tools. It's never
what we plan. It's what evolves from
predecessor, it's what pays

the grocer, doctor, tax collector.
But back to botany, sitting
next to a beautiful woman—
an atmosphere of seeds and saps

made our eyes search each other fast.
Syb and I were married junior
year, back in Bristol. I wanted
one and only guest: Paul, best man.

And best friends did we stay until
the strife when I'd joined men of wife-
lessness, when Sybil'd passed, and lone-
liness came back to me again.

6 *In which Paul tells of college life, becoming a father,*
and reconnecting with Gaddis

At Amherst College I found a whole life
outside Bristol, Tennessee. And I made
the freshman soccer team. It seemed I was

an athlete after all, or is it that
sometimes relativity makes *to seem*
become *to be*? Oh, please, please, don't ask me.

A professor, Rolfe Humphries, embodied
the humanities. A huge imposing
cape he wore when he attended our games.

He liked to think his boys would wax well-round
in facts and fiction, *mens sana in cor-*
pore sano, as the saying went. I

studied Latin, *et cetera, quod erat*
demonstrandum. And Humphries would critique
our matches, ask why the coach kept defense

back so far. Coach Rostas didn't listen
to advice from anyone, and once when
I said, "Coach, I think we'd . . . ," his foreign tongue

spat out: "Don't sink, Pauli Girl, you rueen
zee club." So I decided that I'd best
play mindless soccer and save thinking for

Rolfe Humphries' class and other disciplines
that came my way, until Bristol was
a blurry past including the Speedway, my

Ford Galaxie up on blocks at home, and
Gaddis Tish. College years gave me a voice.
Majoring in Italian language and

lit, I found sounds that filled the gap of my
long-deficient communication skills.
I played the part of Casanova well,

I was told, using "ciao," telling every
girl how "bellissima, carissima"
she was, not to mention knowing ways of

getting each to do things she'd been told to
pay heed to, like when boys said, "Relax and
have a brew or two." Of alcohol, there

was plenty in those days, dark-age days of
no abortions that were legal, just
the botched-up kind. "Knocked up" are the words they used

for girls who found themselves expecting. "Fucked
up" are the words they used for guys who had
to walk the knocked-up down the aisle, which I

did my sophomore year. Her name—no concern.
The marriage like most endured what seemed an
eternity, and heaven it was not.

I sought metaphor of other shores and
mountains, while I tended to Joanna's
diapers and her cries between my thesis

on San Francesco's supplications. "Oh,
Sister Jo," I spoke, "Don't cry, bambina,
my source, soror, O sole mio mine."

Her mother scolded me aloud and hard
for patronizing Jo. "Besides," she'd say,
"don't speak in foreign languages she does

not understand, 'cause Jo's American,
and English is her tongue." So I replied,
smart ass that I was, "Joanna's tongue speaks

not any language under Brother Sun."
By the time Gaddis phoned and asked me to
be "best" man, I was contemplating "worst"

and "least" as the most apt superlatives
to express how I viewed myself as man.
But "Yes!" I shrieked into the phone, "I'll be

your man!" and hitch-hiked alone to Bristol.
Joy I noted in Sybil and Gaddis—
contentment beyond my reach—and saddest

was I thinking of Joanna's future.
I'd find a way to be a loving dad,
avoid remorse, and still get my degree.

At the Tish wedding clarity surfaced:
imminent divorce, alas, left to me.

7 *A flashback, in which Paul reminisces about jumping out of airplanes*

The summer after my divorce I went
back to Amherst College as a senior,
a father, which burden did not preclude

good times—reveling—every now and then.
By May I'd completed all requirements,
and I had time to earn extra money—

anything for Jo, that Sister Moon girl
I adored far more than any creature.
I watched her grow, as if time had doubled.

Jo was meant to be twins. She even had
an extra kidney in her, the Brother
Sun that never rose, but still somehow shone

in Jo. She was always more than one, twice
the baby, twice the toddler, double-child,
the facing open pages of a book,

recto, verso, pages odd and even.
It mattered not. Her take on just about
everything was one of doubling gladness.

At twenty-one, I thought I was adult,
almost, that is to say, I thought I knew
what a guy with a B.A. and a child

had to do. For sure, no law degree, no
Ph.D., for sure no trekking high in
Himalayan nations. Sober thought, that

matriculation. No, the outlook on
my future I adopted was one of
resignation to be a citizen,

though I must say to leave myself no slack
at such a youthful age, i.e., to face
a life of Pollyanna goodness, lacked

even a hint of future fun, and so
I signed up for all the beer I could drink
for a few hours of my daylight time,

helping a professor in his work on
Fear. Beer for Fear—and dollars, too—that might
provide some final grins with college friends.

All we had to do was jump out of a plane
and parachute to terra firma,
then get hooked to wires and plugs, needles on

dials, graphs, oscilloscopes, blood pressure,
heart rates, pulses, saliva, invasive
probes and questions: And *then* how did you feel?

"Scared," I'd say without admitting I had
never flown before that first jump. In fact,
I took off nine times in a plane, never

landing once. And so it was I furthered
humankind's understanding, insofar
as there could be understanding in nine-

teen sixty-five, of what petrifies
the human mind, causes skin to bump and palms
to sweat, valves to leak uncontrollably.

Some months later I had an interview
in Chicago. I took off. I flew. And
then I landed in the plane. It came down

sweet and with a quick squirt of rubber sound.
I jabbed the ribs of him in 15B,
and said, "So, that's a proper touch down. Sure

beats the feet." My seatmate's face, bewildered.

8 *In which Paul relates meeting Lacey*

I was offered the job in Chicago,
insurance. I went to live there, too far
from Jo, who was still in Lee, Mass., growing

like the "weed," indeed a smart, uncommon
girl. I missed her more than I thought ever
possible. "Jo, o sole mio mine,"

I would say by phone before I kissed her
over the wire and she'd say, "Daddy,
Brother Fire, O mio mine, I love you."

Then her mother'd take the phone and harangue
me to cut it out, and I'd just hang up.
All alone, I was that first year in

the city of my Brother Wind. I missed my
kid, and didn't like my job, or people
in it, who lived on actuarials

and rumor. I missed good humor and those
who hashed over the big questions, or what
I called big in those post-diploma days.

Always I was looking for someone to
talk to. Desperate, I attended a
lecture at Northwestern on the myth of

Agdistis and how it was all mixed up
with almonds and wine from Greek and Roman
times down to medieval Italy.

I fell in love with the lecturer, and
asked her out that night. Appalachian girl,
I called her. She grew up in the mountains

looking off toward Caesar's Head just over
the border, North to South Carolina,
close enough to Tennessee. The next night

I asked her to marry me. When it's right,
it's right, all right, and marrying Lacey
was about the most all right thing I've done

all my life. When she got her degree, we
moved to Tennessee, where the "cotton blooms
and blows," she liked to say after meeting

Gaddis, who told her he wasn't much on
mythology, but he could offer her
"The Cremation of Sam McGee" by heart.

That was the start. Gaddis and Sybil—Lace
loved them from that moment on because she
liked anything mismatched, non-sequiturs,

odd tastes, ideas and clothes and funny looks.
She was going to write novels using myth,
which runs deep in all seasons and which casts

reason to the breezes. Myth makes sense and
explains, she'd say, why day makes love to rain
and stars paint skies with plots that end in pain.

I sold insurance—actuarially.
I consulted charts. Not one predicted
Jo's mother would die early. But she did.

Naturally, Jo went through a period
of grieving, being angry and at odds.
She came to live with us, Lacey being

as good a friend as Jo would ever find—
she was fifteen—while Gaddis and Sybil
were just like an uncle and aunt next door.

The twin city, Bristol, that straddled two
states, became home to Jo. She grew into
womanhood, her own twin always with her.

9 In which Lacey, after many years of marriage to Paul,
offers exposition

Why, you might be asking of me, did I spend so
much attention on ancient tomes, whose very spines
were broken and whose words were not in current use
and whose themes of human strengths and weaknesses were
muddled in what certain people call conceits and
canons, words I do not comprehend within their
trend and will not use.
        Well, so I sat and wrote my
fiction, called forth muses, myths that wormed into my
work. And what, you might be asking of me, did your
husband do, that he should take a chicken down to
neighbor Gaddis or, on another night, a stew?

When lovely Sybil "passed" (is how Gaddis said it,
though I never use that word for "died" and I'd not
be caught dead using it), Paul did errands now he'd
packed it in, thrown in the towel, "retired" is
the way they put it in social security crowds.
Jo lived in town—she's such a good daughter to Paul—
but she's very independent and shows no signs
of being swept off her feet by lust or by love.

High in these Tennessee mountains we live among
the oaks, tulip trees, holly, katydids at night
now that it's July. *Our* mountain isn't any
spot of ancient lure like Greece and Italy, where
I'd like to go to find out more about the myth
of Agdistis, but Paul feels no yen to travel,
no desire to give up his cozy placid days.

I should relate only how he handled Gaddis
after Sybil's early death when she turned bluish,
closed her eyes, and her heart stopped beating— just like that.

10 *In which Lacey describes a night Paul took dinner to Gaddis*

It wasn't too far for Paul to walk—albeit
down—to take a dinner that I'd made for Gaddis,
who'd been his friend since kindergarten. Paul would say
he knew him like a brother, though Paul had only
a sister, and she was nothing like a brother,
nothing like a sister for that matter.

                                One night
Paul took chicken and macaroni and cheese with
salad. Gaddis, I knew, would like to have a meal
prepared by someone else. We'd have the same ourselves
that night. We could have asked him to our house, could have
made a festive evening of it, celebrated
something—what, I do not know—but invitation
brings about the need for formality, a change
of clothes, a table set more correctly than I
do when it's just Paul and me. Guests, even best friends,
preclude what we always do—skipping a dessert—
when we're alone. And going sans baguette and beurre.

"Lacey," Paul called, walking in perhaps more quickly
than he might've under ordinary circum-
stances on an uphill trek.

While I poured him
a glass of pinot grigio from Alto Adige,
his favorite white for under ten, he in a way
exploded with the Gaddis tale.

"I took the food,"
he said, "and walked into his kitchen. What a mess
I found! Smelly garbage! Gross raucous cesspool of
rinds and weeds, greening carcasses, gizzards on
a counter waiting for the drive to the dump. But who
to put it in the can was there? I, sure as hell,
wouldn't take it anywhere.

And so as I left
the chicken on the kitchen table, I could hear
a voice down the hall in another room, the voice
of Gaddis, or near-Gaddis. It was softer, more
rhythmic, still the Gaddis voice I knew. Did it speak
poetry? Did I dare shout, 'Gaddis, is that you?'"

"So what did you do?" I asked Paul, who was by now
clearly fixed in another place of memory
of what he'd found and what he'd done.

"I tiptoed down
the hall," he said, "toward the room where I heard the voice,
and there sat Gaddis in Sybil's dress, his back to
me and he reciting in a soft but surely
Gaddis voice, of all the goddamnedest oddities—
oh, you can guess—'The Cremation of Sam McGee.'"

11 *In which Paul relates how he decided he and Lacey should write Gaddis off and leave the country*

"He's crazy," I told Lacey, "a pervert,
a queer cross-dresser, whom I thought I knew
after all these years. Gotta have a brew."

She'd poured a pinot grigio for me, but
I couldn't face the foppery and found
a long-neck Bud left-over from last June.

Lacey left me alone in our kitchen
with my thoughts to order and collect. She
hates it when I say things I will regret.

But in my state of shock, my mind made up,
I sighed, "Leave Gaddis/Gladys to his skirts,
to his recitations of Cremation

poetry. Lacey and I will travel
Greece and Italy, forget this fool who's
been our friend, who must've found relief when

Sybil died, then slightly nervous, begowned,

began reciting Robert Service. And

I'll say not one word more to him. I'll tell

Lacey to do or not to do the same,

but I'd bet a million bucks or five that

she bids Gaddis a goodbye or two." So

forthwith we went to Greece, where Lacey looked

into the Agdistis myth. We toured Crete,

Delphi, climbed Parnassus, looked out over

Levadia, the plain where cotton grows

the way it does, or did, in Tennessee.

Lacey seemed to look beyond, wistfully,

but sort of cheerfully. It reminded

her of Sam McGee. She missed her buddy,

my one-time friend, smiled when she thought of him.

I saw it in her face when she'd become

about Agdistis newly enlightened—

his/her mother/self. Hermaphrodite, and

she took long notes on the story. How it

fit into her novel, how it was

part of Gaddis somehow. But I said, brusquely,

"Don't say that person's name to me again."

12 *Lacey's research notes for her novel*

Short-stemmed cotton grows many months in Copaïs
Valley, once lake, then plain. To drain, Mycenean
engineers figured how—but filled again. Water
can't be tamed—marshes grow back like bamboo & cane.
Now beautiful plain again, has been since '20s.
Cotton as in Tennessee grows Greek soft thorny
plenty—Turkish trade—Cybele's wildness begins
on Mt. Ida. Too close she sits to errant seeds
of Zeus—the cad. He bandies sperm about and laughs
when she conceives, but people and gods see her as
mom. Soon she births not fish nor fowl called Agdistis.
Hermaphrodite, w *his* vagina, *her* penis,
anomalies catch eye and ear of deities
on mountaintop—cliffs & caves & pools, & wine runs
like salmon. Drunken frenzies churn waters that mix
w alcohol—till one day he/she, Agdistis,
falls asleep. Jokester gods tie his/her prick to tree,
& so when Agdistis shifts, he becomes all she.
Where the member lands, an almond tree—called "crazy"
for flowering in winter mindless of the chill—
grows up erect recklessly in true family
tradition. So when maiden daughter of river
god—Nana—sits beneath it, an almond locates

just the place to hide: her reddish cave—& throbbing,

too. Out slips boy Attis in nine months' time. His looks

could kill—falls in love w Agdistis, who by now

passes for Cybele & all is mixed up in

pots of seeds & nuts & gods & sons & mothers,

daughters granddaughters grandsons & goddesses &

Greeks & Turks & Romans & those whosoever

at future times will need cotton gowns to wear in

temples & in market places. So interwove

those threads of Copaïs and Tennessee, other

places west and east, & mother to all creatures.

N.B. All creatures inside all creatures.

Each the other. Male/female, tree/squirrel, friend/stranger.

13 *In which Gaddis comments on his neighbors, Paul and Lacey*

I've watched Lacey and Paul deal
with his retirement. Lacey gets
hung up on her novel based on
the myth of who? Yes, Agdistis—

that's it. I know the name perhaps
because I share the g, the a,
the d, i, the s, or maybe
because the story's so bizarre,

he's being she's, and then she's he's,
sons becoming idol-mothers,
lovers all mixed up in classic
sacred mountains where nature rules.

Sybil died without much warning.
Paul got me through it. Later he'd
come over with a meal or just
to talk, to shoot the breeze, to have

a pop, just like old times, and twice
we went to the track. The thought of
Brenda Lee made us say things you
say only to a friend. Meanwhile,

we had to catch up on NASCAR,
new names, new brands, new rules and stats.
Paul was in heaven at the track.
Wistful leaves not the human heart.

If anyone had asked me what
Paul would do when he retired,
I'd have said he'd get himself mired
in things of Italy, his dear

St. Francis of Assisi, who
would harken back to Paul's B.A.
at Amherst, when he learned to speak
Italian and studied all

the poets from Francesco on to
Ungaretti (see how he taught
me?)—but that's the extent of my
learnedness. No facility

for languages, pity, or for
a poetry that doesn't rhyme
for that matter. Paul's always said
I should've lived in other times.

That's why I felt so sad when they
left me high and dry, no goodbye,
and flew to Greece and Italy.
I saw their darkened quiet house.

How was I to know it was my
dressing up in Sybil's clothes and
reciting "Sam McGee" aloud
that brought about these distresses?

(I do it now for pay these days.)
How I missed my friend and Lacey.

14 *In which Paul describes an ever-deepening melancholy during the trip abroad*

The happier Lacey got about her
novel's plot falling into place—and this
because of what she'd learned in Greece and how

she'd held it up as a mirror to our
life in the Tennessee mountains, being
next door to Gaddis, who, she tried to say,

was lonely when his Sybil died and he
had no other way to keep her with him
than to let her dresses surround him tight—

the sadder I became. Not only had
I mocked my dearest friend for having gone
weird if not downright queer on me, but I'd

abandoned him, absented myself from
the very sight of him and yet I saw
this hardly causing my despondency.

In Italy Lacey drove, while I sat
in the passenger seat brooding, moping
from hotel to hotel, while she tried to

find out what was bugging me, and I just
sank my chin deeper into my collar,
fixed my eyes on nothing, as we wound through

Lombardia and through Piemonte.
Lacey told me she would take me to stark
tranquility: beautiful Lake Orta.

15 *In which Paul describes ascending with Lacey the
Sacro Monte dedicated to St. Francis of Assisi in Orta
San Giulio, Italy, and having the closest thing he'd ever
have to a religious experience*

We got to Orta in the afternoon.
Lacey said exercise would do me good.
So we walked up to the Sacro Monte,

which was part-park, part-church, part-mystery.
As we went through a gate I saw the old
familiar poetry of St. Francis

on a wall, Brother Sun, Sister Moon.
Wind on my face felt like a hand. Lacey brushed
the hair out of my eyes, and then she said,

"Here is the first chapel. Let's see what it
depicts." There we were, beginning the climb.
You start with Francesco's birth. I thought of

Joanna. How full of awe I was when
she was born. It made me think of Gaddis,
how he and Sybil loved her as their own.

But I told myself to silence Gaddis
in my head and just follow the chapels
that line the road on both sides, as it climbs

and climbs and climbs to where St. Francis dies.
You walk from one chapel to the other,
peering in at scenes from the saint's life and

getting a sense of him, who renounced wealth
and family to commune with the poor,
with Clare and fauna-flora, to cherish

nature, sun, wind, moon, brothers, sisters all.
He disrobed in public. Naked he took
a vow of poverty. He attracted

followers. He loved Clare very much. "Did
they sleep together?" Lacey asked me, since
in her line of work things like that happen.

I did not answer. An unfamiliar
breath was touching me. The chapels were gifts
in the fifteenth, sixteenth centuries from

wealthy Ortans, who saw fit to buy their
way into the paradise of the day.
They hired architects to design their

monument, a sculptor, too, to people
it with terra cotta figures that had
faces, clothes, from contemporary times.

And so St. Francis stood and sometimes sat
wearing anachronistic shoes or hat,
that did not detract from my renewed love

of Assisi's *poverello*, when at
the last chapel I peered in at his death
scene and saw myself and Gaddis, or was

it Lacey's face I saw? Were we terra
cotta statues, dressed as Piedmont peasants
of sixteenth-century style? Lacey/Gaddis

seemed to be my wife. We were on-lookers,
townspeople, witnessing a man's dying,
stigmata filled with dark blood in his hands,

in his side, and in his feet. My body
shook and shook, and shaking wildly chilly
uncharacteristically I fell

to painless knees. Never had I felt such
ecstasy, except when I laid eyes on
Jo. So young was I, and now so old.

Looking through my tears I felt connection
to my daughter, to my wife, to my youth,
to my friend, and the silence of statues.

16 *In which Lacey reveals Paul's stock car reverie,*
recovery, and remedy: the Nascro Monte

I took Paul down to the edge of the lake, holding
his hand, on rough earth, reversing his life down through
the infant's birth and through the gate to the village.
Paul was quieter than I'd ever known him. We looked
toward the Island of Silence, where nuns scurry
furtively between stone buildings, never speaking.
And finally, Paul said to me calmly that he
felt a certain humility. In our state of
quiet, side by side on a bench of grace, did we
contemplate things that fell beyond all our knowledge:
he said he'd made a big mistake to abandon
Gaddis after all the years of being comrades,
neighbors, confidantes, sounding boards, to each other.
He didn't know why he did it. Death, faith perhaps
are what Paul focused on.
                              The air of Orta was
still, when out of nowhere, as if a squall brought
a monster from the lake, seventeen stock cars, Fiats,
all colors, each with a number, in line stormed through
tiny Orta. Paul awoke from his silent trance.
The overwhelming organic sound prompted his
mouth to open into one huge smile and the word:

"NASCAR." He shouted, "NASCAR," screamed it out into

the lake over the noise of the cars. "NASCAR!" he

exclaimed. "St. Francis, thanks, oh, thanks, for the silence

of this sacred place that made me think of NASCAR

as my cure."

        "It's getting cold," I said. "Let's go to

our room and toast the Sacred Mount."

                "Sacro Monte,"

he corrected me, and then in afterthought he

fairly whispered, "Nascro Monte."

                To our hotel

we walked, but when we turned on CNN we knew

just why forces were at play with Paul: Dale Earnhardt,

dead that day, an engine cut down, choked into

the silence of the very island in the shadow

of St. Francis, the eighteenth of February

two thousand one A.D., or in the common era.

17 *In which Paul describes their return from Italy to Tennessee*

I've never been a man of easy words—
just ask my Lace whose words appear so fit
upon the page—but I'll try—at my age—

to chronicle the time from when we drove
to Malpensa Airport and took off for
home, demanding only safe flight and smooth

landing, which of course I venerated
like a man who'd had no candy as
a child and every time he saw a lolli-

pop he salivated. Driving away
from Orta and the island, our rented
car became a cocoon of happiness,

or if not happiness, of contentment
at least, a shared glee that made both Lacey
and me flush and blush with rediscovered

comfort in each other's presence. When this
happened, only then I realized how
the peace of delight had been missing from our

union, that bond of ecstatic lovers.
There was in Italy that year a strong
and fervent campaign for Padre Pio

to become a saint, arcane practice that
it is. Candidates must be proven to
have miracles under their belt to make

sainthood. Such a miracle took place in
Orta when Pio's face appeared upon
the side of a building just opposite

San Rocco's little church. But when I looked
at what was thought to be his face, I did
not see what others seemed to see. Perhaps

my faith was not yet at that exact point
of runneth over. But I digress too
much.   I must get back to our plane's return

home. I was so full of renewal and
resolve to make things right. And so it was
that our landing became a symbol for

our life. Touch-down brought determination
to Lacey to complete her Agdistis
novel. And me? I would build my Nascro

Monte on our hill. Touch-down brought me back
to earth where I'd not been for years, as if
I'd died without goodbye to all I loved.

18 *In which Paul contemplates friendship*

St. Francis never would have shunned his friends,
as I had so gravely to Gaddis done.
I felt remorse, I felt regret, and yet

it took some time to go to him and ask
forgiveness. In fact, I never frankly
went to tell him that I understood him

better now that I knew something more of
what it meant to be woman or a man,
creature, god, or mute inanimate thing;

what it meant to be a breathing, living
being climbing to the top of any
mountain in the world, Parnassus, Ida

or a Sacro Monte in Italy;
or a being walking on a wide plain
of cotton plants in Greece or Tennessee.

Respect for history had evaded
me, and so I was imprisoned in my
own prejudging mind, which did not let me

cherish memory as it should be loved
where a friend is concerned. I'd hurt Gaddis,
my friend. When I accounted for the share

of him that was inside of me—this was
when Lacey and I sat down in Orta
looking off toward the Island of Silence—

I heard the roar of race cars. Whether there
were truly cars that day I'll never know.
I've been known to see things that are not there.

What I do know is that Gaddis's face
appeared on the wall of an Ortan house
as if he were a candidate for saint

performing a requisite miracle.
I asked the face for forgiveness. I gave
thanks to the sacred air that embraced me.

19 *In which Jo does a double-take at the progress of the Nascro Monte*

My father called a back-hoe man to dig
nine holes, a tenth one smaller to hold a flame.
They took about a day or two to dig
but Dad then had to contour them by digging
with a shovel, so the cars could stand
exactly at the proper angle. Dig
the backhoe did, and then my dad did dig
for weeks, and there were mounds around of earth
to pack the cars in, tightly wrapped in dignity,
forever revved or idling in place,
they aimed toward a high and better place.

The vintage cars came from wreckage places,
rusty, yes, but beautiful and dignified,
two Fords, three Chevrolets. Dad replaced
some parts, repainted their front ends, and placed
them nose-up. Three Dodges, too, with flames
decal'd red hot, he lowered into place.
The angle for the eight racecars in place
is sixty degrees, no more, for them to stand
leaning like some rockets in their stand,
though these missiles will never leave the place

Dad put them in, the back-hoed mountain earth,
burial holes in racers' and Dad's earth.

He shoveled and he packed the summer earth
to fill the hole, the hollows, empty places
around the lines of automotive earth-
bound designs (better left unearthed),
yet Dad did not have very far to dig
inside his head to know they were on Earth
the most divine designs. And then the earthen—
terra cotta—figures shone flamboyant
real at night, all lit by floodlight flames.
Allison, Cale, and Junior Johnson, not yet in earth
themselves, and Darrell Waltrip, Pearson stand
as statue-selves beside their racecar stands.

Petty, handsome sculpted image standing
there and looking glad to be on earth,
seemed as he did the day of his last stand
in '92, retired with the standings
of a King, two hundred wins, first-place.
My dad has made me know and understand
the extra awe he feels when standing
near those deceased but not forgot and not ig-

nored, not deplored at all for "digging
their own grave," as those who cannot stand
the racers and the sport that they enflame
declare. Just think of Fireball Roberts' flames.

His name from pitching came from which he flamed
out, while racing he could not withstand.
So when he died a death among the flames,
the irony, the fiery, the flaming
injustices, unfairnesses on Earth
symbolized those who end in flames,
sadly headed for the hall-of-flame.
Father, son, my dad did warmly place
at Nascro Monte's peak, the special place
for Earnhardts and a bright eternal flame:
Dale, Senior, Number 3, the living digit,
Dale, Junior, Number 8, a fading digit.

In June the backhoe first began to dig.
By August Dad had everything in place.
Autumn's here with all its smells of earth,
and cars like flowers grow half within the earth
atop Dad's hill. The Nascro Monte stands:
a beacon, the immortal NASCAR flame.

20 *In which Lacey recaps where things stood after she and Paul returned to Tennessee*

My novel's progress echoed Paul's Nascro Monte.
Sure, each had its moments of "not"—not pleasant, not
overcoming obstacles (temporarily),
but whereas mine were mental "not's," writer's blocks, of
clots of knots within my veins that got all twisted
'round the myths and who was who and who begat whom
or sprang up from an almond, Paul's not's were cinder
blocks and drains, questions about mortar, how much sand,
how much cement, how many stations would there be?
Who had a backhoe and who could dig the holes and
what junkyard had the cars needed, and what about
eternal flame? Is eternity forever?
As for my novel, well, it was hard to pull it all
together. Hero Agdistis symbolized
humankind as I saw it then, though that will change
with time, for nothing stays the same. And my lesser
characters kept doing things I'd not expect or
worse. Poetry it's not. Yet I am certain when
a subject is just right for prose, and when it's right
for verse.
      And next door there was Gaddis, who put on
dresses and recited "Sam McGee." In fact, we

three were back to what it was before we forsook
our friend, who merely wanted his dead wife to put
her arms around him again and to close him tight
in her clothes with all her might and her lovely scent.
"Sam McGee" is part of this in a way I don't
fully understand. I only know there's laughter
mixed with history mixed with pathos mixed with longing.

I know the three of us in isolation, did—
Paul, Gaddis, I—our thing, but we were always drawn
into centrifugal shared elation. Gaddis
helped me move my plot along and to develop
my characters so Agdistis soon was rendered
less mythical, a creature to be palpated.
My hero/heroine became so real in fact
I could almost see her or sometimes him beyond
the pages that I typed. One night feeling relieved,
I invited Gaddis for dinner (I had made
apple pie) to celebrate. He came in Sybil's
Turkish caftan with the red sash and velvet shoes.

It was the evening when Paul came back having spelled
with hubcaps the name of Kannapolis (Earnhardt's
place of birth). With this Paul was so pleased he contra-

danced up hill, then down, then up, even with bad knees.
"Lacey, Lacey!" he called out, not knowing Gaddis
was in our house. "You have to see the hubcaps. They're . . ."
And he stopped in his boots, taking in the caftan.
"Hello, Paul," Gaddis said. "I saw the hubcaps. They
are perfect there with Earnhardt's baby photographs.
The whole thing spells Kannapolis. Well done, my man."

Paul sat down. I thought better of Pinot Grigio
and grabbed a Bud for him. "Gaddis says he has some
news for us, Paul."
    "News, Gaddis? What's your news, old friend?"
I began to breathe more easily when I heard
that "old friend." And Gaddis shifted in his chair in
a reassuring pose of comfort. "I'm getting
married again," he said. Paul sucked on the Bud. "It's
someone who comes often to my performances.
Actually she's a bit younger than me. She's
forty, actually, daughter of an old friend
of Sybil's actually."
    "Who?" Paul asked

                      "Aggie."

"Aggie who?"
    "Aggie Dee."

              "Why, Gaddis, that's great news,"

I said.

"But that's not all," he said. "We'd like to be married in October at the Nascro Monte."
Paul put his lips to the bottle and left them there, one long pull. October 4, St. Francis's Feast
Then he spoke with a smile on his face: "This never could have happened, never, actuarially."

Two children—one male, known as Sate, half-god half-goat,

the other one female, Taury, half-mortal half-

horse—were playing on the slopes of Mount Parnassus.

Each wanted to be Zeus. Sate said, "You be Zeus first."

Taury galloped high onto a rock where she reared,

beat her chest and called loud for thunder and lightning

that did not appear in the placid sky above.

"Zeus doesn't like our game," Sate said. "Why?" Taury asked.

He didn't answer. In stead, on her cheek he put

his hoof gently, said what Zeus thought didn't matter.

"Now you be Zeus," Taury said, neighing quietly.

Sate jumped and quickly ate a prickly pear. He found

an apple and gave it to Taury, knowing well

as part-mortal, she couldn't eat a prickly pear.

Before Sate could assume the role of Zeus, they saw

a woman in a black cape coming down the path.

"Zeus does not want you to be playing with a horse,

a mere mortal, and a female at that," she said

to Sate. Taury heard her and said to her, "Old bitch,

take off that cloak, that I might see your face." The old

woman pulled the cape around her tightly. Sate pulled

at it. As it fell from the woman's broad shoulders,

she changed into a scorpion. Neither Sate nor
Taury was scared. "It's Zeus!" they cried in unison.
"I'll step on him," Taury said. "He is poisonous
but can't hurt us." And as she pounded the scorpion,
it became the spitting image of her father.

"My child," he said, "I don't want to hurt you. I loved
your mother, a stunning mare, who gave birth to you
and galloped away. Now you have Sate, a friend, good
and loyal, kind, one who brings divine miracles
to your friendship, just as you bring the miracles
of mortals to it. Not one more than the other."

Taury looked at her father. "You are really Zeus,
aren't you?" she asked him, as he shook his head and said:

"We are creatures, mixtures of bloods and skins, fractions
of divinity and mortality, muscled
heartbeats, who earth-bound look beyond the pasture gate.
The forces in our lives change constantly. I *am*
your father now. But now I leave. Go with your friend."
And the man collapsed into a marble gravestone,
white roadside marker, on which Taury put her hoof.
"Good bye, Father," she whispered, turning back to Sate,

who watched the fond scene between man and horse-daughter.
"Your turn to be Zeus," she called out, trotting away
from where her father's apparition had just been.

22 *In which Lacey and Paul hash over the wedding*

It couldn't have been more beautiful or solemn
all those half-sunk cars festooned with chrysanthemums
at a time of year when colors begin to mash
into one winter hue, and autumn's almost passed
the prayer-wheel swirl of wind, orange, brittle yellow.

Lacey, you're still in a sentimental
mood, left over from the wedding, aren't you?

Well, I doubt the Nascro Monte will ever see
a ceremony like it in such company.

I disagree. It's just the spiritual
spot I dreamed about. And any ritual
would be fitting in that most sacred place.

A funeral?

Perhaps, or a baptism.

Do you know something I don't know about Aggie?
Didn't she look beautiful in that *peau de soie*?
Where did she ever find such a dress? So perfect.

And Gaddis—how 'bout that fellow, Lacey?

Gorgeous, wasn't he? After all our worrying!

I swear, I thought he'd wear some goddam dress
of Sybil's with sequins. Instead he walks
the hill to Earnhardt's Chevy in new pants,
blue blazer, and a tie. I thought I'd die.
He stepped right out of 1965.

You looked pretty fine, yourself, Reverend Paul, waiting
at Earnhardt's Chevy in that Greek cotton chiton.

Those damned credentials that I got on line
in cyberspace from god knows where. "Preacher
of the Internet celebrates nuptials
for friend in open air." St. Francis would
approve, I have no doubt. I felt him there
high up on our Nascro Monte. And Jo,
my very Clare, enclosed us in her arms.

23 *In which Gaddis describes his bride, as she walked alone up to the top of the Nascro Monte*

She had no father or mother
to walk beside her or keep her
steady on the uphill climb I'd
done ahead of her in time to

turn and see my bride, my Aggie
take her first steps through the Gate of
Kannapolis. The vision was
beyond all loveliness and peace.

Tall and thin, Aggie wore the dress
my mother married in, the dress
my father caught me in, the dress
he kissed me in, the dress I'd worn

whenever I felt lonely as
an only child, and torn apart,
the *peau de soie* that held me in
its sleeves and soothed my broken heart.

Aggie walked between the Chevies
and the Fords, the Dodges, and
the terra cotta men that made cars
run on speedways—like disciples

who could spread the word faster than
a lightning bolt, a radio,
a circuitry of messages,
a Bible with Apocrypha.

I stood next to my best friend Paul.
At last the rift that severed us
had passed for good. He truly seemed
to beam beside Dale Earnhardt's car.

In my lapel a gardenia
whispered hello to those ready
to hear sincerity of touch.
It would brown by the end of day,

but the scent would remember white
velvet petals. Lacey and Jo
stood on either side of Paul and
me, waiting for my Aggie Dee

to reach the top. And when she did,
I kissed her lips and took her hand.
We faced the Reverend Paul, who looked
the part in something Sybil would

have worn, a flowing robe of sorts,
how strange the tables turn. Paul cued
Jo to do her part, in which she—
with all of her duality—

pulled us into one with NASCAR,
almonds for fertility, myth,
St. Francis of Assisi, love
and hate and "Sam McGee," as if

another voice inside of her
spoke up simultaneously.
The power of a sacred place
through Jo us all embraced.

24 *In which Jo recites a poem at the wedding*

There are strange things done in the name of Sun
  That sole mio mine.
There's nothing hazy—or am I crazy?—
  'bout Sun's eternal shine.
Now, weather's moods are understood
  with measuring tools in place,
but when St. Francis wrote his canticle
  he did it for us and Lace.

With praise begun for Brother Sun,
whose rays distressed his eyes,
he showed the love, the romance of
a lover's warm replies.
You, Brother Sun, who bring the day,
are splendor more than fine.
The fire and light, your gentle might,
are radiance divine.

His praise communed with Stars and Moon,
Sisters precious, fair,
and Brother Wind, with whom he twinned
calm and stormy Air.
It was arctic air that caused despair

in Sam McGee's quest for gold.
He whined and moaned and cursed the worst
and died from polar cold.

Well, the poem says that he dropped dead,
his body frozen stiff.
But Brother Fire thawed him entirely
and brought him back to life.
Which leads the way to Nascro Monte,
sacred mountain space,
where Gaddis T. and Aggie Dee,
eternal flame in place,

have joined their souls, forever hold
each other, he and she,
and will think over this October
as Francis' and McGee's
and Dale's and Junior Johnson's doom,
Sybil's, and all the others,
Agdistis, making sense at last,
my unnamed blessed mother.

They left this world's chaotic swirl
by Sister Death's affection,

but temporary, all contrary,
she arranged their resurrections.
Now dearly beloved, here up above
next to Number Three,
the plain below awaits us, so
in cotton we will be.

Author's Note

There's a little bit of method to these syllabic verses. I picked eight syllables for Gaddis's lines because of his love of the ballad; ten for Paul because of his seemingly mundane profession, evoking perhaps our own iambic pentameter cadences. And Lacey, being a novelist and therefore the wordiest of the three, got twelve syllables. As for Jo, the duality with which she was born lent itself unabashedly to a double-sestina in No. 19.

Anne Harding Woodworth is the author of two books of poetry and two chapbooks. Her essays and poetry are published widely in U.S. and Canadian journals, as well as at several sites online. She has an MFA in poetry from Fairleigh Dickinson University and divides her time between Western North Carolina and Washington, D.C., where she is a member of the Poetry Board at the Folger Shakespeare Library.

LaVergne, TN USA
03 April 2010
178012LV00004B/3/P